Headline Series

No. 284   FOREIGN POLICY ASSOCIATION $4.00

Gorbachev's Foreign Policy
How Should the United States Respond?

by Robert Legvold
and
The Task Force on Soviet New Thinking

Cover Design: Ed Bohon

May/June 1987
Published April 1988

The Authors

ROBERT LEGVOLD is director of the W. Averell Harriman Institute for Advanced Study of the Soviet Union at Columbia University, and was a member of the Task Force on Soviet New Thinking. Joseph Nye, director of the Center for Science and International Affairs at Harvard University, and Whitney MacMillan, chairman and chief executive officer of Cargill, Inc., were cochairmen of the Task Force. The Task Force's report, *How Should America Respond to Gorbachev's Challenge?* was published October 10, 1987, by the Institute for East-West Security Studies in New York City.

Robert Legvold

The Foreign Policy Association
The Institute for East-West Security Studies

This publication is a joint effort of the Foreign Policy Association and the Institute for East-West Security Studies. FPA is a private, not-for-profit, nonpartisan educational organization whose purpose is to stimulate wider interest and more effective participation in world affairs. The Institute for East-West Security Studies is the only permanent center bringing East and West together in sustained dialogue, study and research on security issues. Established in 1981 as an independent not-for-profit international initiative, the Institute works to identify policy-oriented options to enhance stability, reduce the dangers of conflict and expand East-West cooperation. The authors are responsible for the accuracy and the views expressed in this HEADLINE SERIES.

HEADLINE SERIES (ISSN 0017-8780) is published five times a year, January, March, May, September and November, by the Foreign Policy Association, Inc., 729 Seventh Ave., New York, N.Y. 10019. Chairman, Robert V. Lindsay; President, John W. Kiermaier; Editor in Chief, Nancy L. Hoepli; Senior Editor, Ann R. Monjo; Associate Editor, K. M. Rohan. Subscription rates, $15.00 for 5 issues; $25.00 for 10 issues; $30.00 for 15 issues. Single copy price $4.00. Discount 25% on 10 to 99 copies; 30% on 100 to 499; 35% on 500 to 999; 40% on 1,000 or more. Payment must accompany order for $8 or less. Add $1.50 for postage. Second-class postage paid at New York, N.Y. POSTMASTER: Send address changes to HEADLINE SERIES, Foreign Policy Association, 729 Seventh Ave., New York, N.Y. 10019. Copyright 1988 by Foreign Policy Association, Inc. Composed and printed at Science Press, Ephrata, Pennsylvania.

Library of Congress Catalog Card No. 88-80338
ISBN 0-87124-118-8

Introduction*
by the Task Force
on Soviet New Thinking

After three years in power, Soviet leader Mikhail S. Gorbachev has made it clear to both domestic and foreign audiences that he intends to carry out a thorough restructuring of the Soviet system in an effort to make the Soviet economy capable of effectively assimilating the opportunities offered by contemporary science, technology and methods of management. Concerned that the Soviet system inherited from the Brezhnev period had become ossified, with consequences for the U.S.S.R.'s international standing as well as its material well-being, the new Soviet leadership has called into question a whole series of institutional arrangements and attitudes—ranging from a strictly centralized economic management system to an often militarized foreign

---

*From the report of the Task Force on Soviet New Thinking. Minor changes in style and punctuation have been made for consistency.

policy—that has provided the foundation for Soviet policy for nearly 60 years. Not content with the kind of administrative adjustments that ever since Khrushchev's time have been the Soviet substitute for meaningful reform, Gorbachev has repeatedly underscored the need for structural economic reform and, just as important, for social and political reforms in order to sustain the economy over the long run.

The sheer magnitude of change that is currently being attempted in a country of the size and international import of the U.S.S.R. would of itself demand the world's attention. The interest of the international community is further engaged by the emphasis the Gorbachev leadership has placed on aligning Soviet foreign policy more closely with long-term internal requirements, particularly the modernization of the economy. This has entailed an evident rethinking in Soviet policy circles about the requirements of foreign and security policy in an age characterized by mutual nuclear deterrence and global interdependence.

When Gorbachev became general secretary in March 1985, many Western observers assumed that, due to the pressing nature of domestic affairs—especially in the economy—Soviet foreign policy would show little innovation at first. Yet Gorbachev's actions and statements, particularly since the 27th Party Congress in February/March 1986, suggest that his foreign policy perspective differs significantly from that of his predecessors. While change is currently often more noticeable on the conceptual than the policy level, the new Soviet leadership seems to recognize that serious economic and technological deficiencies jeopardize the U.S.S.R.'s international position, and that reversing these trends requires not only major economic modernization but also many new foreign policy approaches.

It is important when considering the foreign policy implications of Gorbachev's initiatives and statements not to focus unduly on the concept of "new thinking" as such, which has been advanced by Gorbachev and his associates as a general rubric for the general secretary's approach to international affairs. Any new thinking takes place within a historical context of adaptation by the Soviet leadership to external realities. It is this broader

Nikita S. Khrushchev opens the historic 20th Party Congress in 1956, at which he denounced Stalin. A former speechwriter for Khrushchev and supporter of Gorbachev's reforms recently wrote that Khrushchev risked his life when he attacked Stalin.

pattern, and not any particular slogan, that should be the focus of Western attention.

In many ways, the world view that Gorbachev and his colleagues have been formulating represents an explicit crystallization of tendencies that have been present—often in piecemeal form—in Soviet policy circles since Nikita Khrushchev's anti-Stalin speech at the 20th Party Congress in 1956. But the resultant synthesis of new and traditional elements constitutes a distinctly "Gorbachevian" perspective which seeks to integrate domestic and foreign policy in a mutually reinforcing combination.

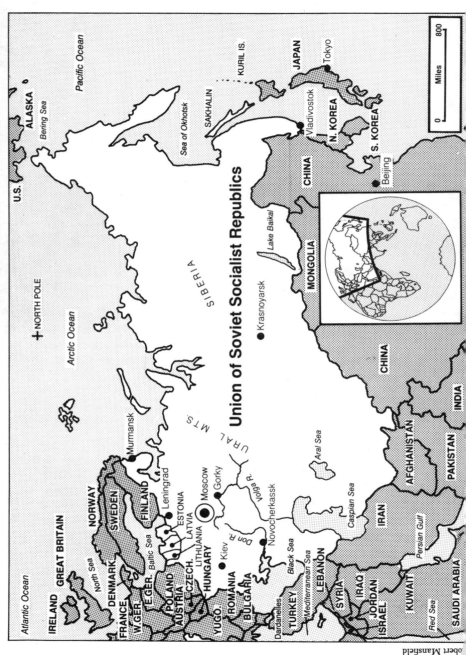

Union of Soviet Socialist Republics

Robert Mansfield

Gorbachev's 'New Thinking'
by Robert Legvold

Hardly anyone any longer questions the scale of the revolution Mikhail Gorbachev wants to visit on an ossified Soviet system. The quarrels are over his chances of success and what the outcome, one way or another, will mean for Western interests. In fact, however, far more important to those who live outside the Soviet Union is the revolution he may or may not be bringing to his country's foreign policy. His struggle to change the Soviet Union, while fascinating and even historic, will not matter much to the rest of the world unless Soviet behavior abroad changes too.

Gorbachev and his people say that they are ready to reform foreign as well as internal policy and to engage in what they call "new political thinking" about international affairs. Indeed, they have been impatiently urging the United States and other critical Western nations to join them.

But what is the West being asked to join? Is something happening on the Soviet side, or is the new political thinking a convenient but empty, maybe even a cynical, slogan? People, let alone whole governments, do not suddenly begin thinking differently because someone announces they should.

New thinking implies a change of mind. (The "new thinking" label itself almost certainly confounds understanding more than it helps, and it might be better to set it aside and look for formulations that have more solidity and focus. Or perhaps the phrase should simply be seen as having the same force as slogans used by American Presidents, say the New Deal or the New Frontier.) Has Gorbachev changed his thinking about the Soviet role abroad? Even to the degree he has, can the same be said for the rest of the regime or for the majority of those who have a hand in shaping Soviet foreign policy? The outsider can be forgiven if all the Soviet pronouncements and exhortations sound a bit like propaganda.

The outsider must also recognize, however, that governments and the men who form them do modify their ideas as the world evolves. Over the years Soviet leaders have allowed their views to change on many subjects. V. I. Lenin, it should be remembered, believed he was making a revolution that would spark revolutions throughout Europe and, in the process, destroy all the traditional features of relations among nation-states—wars, colonialism, power politics as well as diplomatic conventions. But within months, Lenin began making his peace with a rather different reality and joined the game of nations, acknowledging, in effect, the ascendancy of the international order of his day over revolution.

Thirty-five years ago Soviet leaders believed that war among the great powers was not only conceivable but inevitable and, indeed, that out of war revolution would prosper. But nuclear weapons changed this. Nikita S. Khrushchev, the first of the Soviet leaders to live with these weapons, suppressed the notion of the inevitability of war and, indeed, made avoiding war an imperative of policy.

Not so many decades ago Soviet leaders believed in a cohesive socialist bloc of nations, responsive to Soviet leadership, respectful of the Soviet example and helpless before Soviet power. ("I will shake my little finger," Joseph Stalin said when the Yugoslavs defied his attempt to absorb them in the East European bloc in 1948, "and [Yugoslav leader Marshal] Tito will be no more.") No longer. Soviet leaders years ago gave up this simple faith and have gradually reconciled themselves to a degree of diversity and disarray within the world of socialism vastly different from anything Stalin could ever have imagined.

Not so far in the past, Soviet leaders, most notably Khrushchev, believed the newly decolonized nations of the Third World would turn their backs on their former colonial masters and align themselves in steadily increasing number with progressive socialist-led forces. No longer. Over the last quarter century, Soviet leaders have come to have a far more nuanced view of change in the Third World and a far greater sensitivity to the impediments to the spread of revolution. The list goes on.

To doubt the capacity of Soviet leaders to change their minds, therefore, reveals a frail grasp of history. Rather than being put off by the Madison Avenue quality of Gorbachev's phrase, one would be wiser to consider the possibility that for real and good reasons the evolution of concepts continues, not as a sudden break with the past but as a natural progression.

When ideas begin to change, the difference is not always immediately evident in altered behavior. But eventually the inertial force of habit and inherited policy is overcome and a revised understanding of external realities alters practical priorities. In the weave of word and deed, the character of change can be many things. At times when words change it may only be a matter of tactics or atmospherics or style. At other times it may be a matter of strategy—that is, a reordering of priorities and a rethinking of the game plan. The change that matters most is in aspirations and aims, in the way the national interest and the requirements of policy are defined. From change at this level, a whole chain of adjustments in agenda and behavior follows. Difficult as it may be, determining what kind of change is currently under way in the Soviet Union behind the facade of the new thinking is unquestionably of enormous importance to those on the outside.

Domestic Priorities

Gorbachev from the beginning has made it plain that the problems facing him and his colleagues at home take precedence over, indeed dictate, Soviet engagement in the outside world. At the 27th Party Congress (see appendix on page 40 for segments of the report Gorbachev delivered) and in nearly every subsequent major foreign policy speech, he has made some reference such as the following: "Before my people, before those present and before the whole world, I state with full responsibility that our foreign policy is today to a greater extent than ever before determined by domestic policy, by our interest in concentrating our efforts on constructive activities aimed at improving our country. And that is why we need a lasting peace, predictability and constructiveness in international relations." Considering the scale of the problems he confronts, most observers assume that these are more than just words.

Gorbachev does not, of course, mean to suggest that the Soviet Union no longer cares to behave like a superpower or that his country's internal ills have destroyed its mission abroad. But he does seem to believe that his intellectual and political energy must be applied to turning the tide at home, and that his success will depend in part on avoiding excessive foreign policy distractions, whether in the form of nonessential entanglements or a convulsive surge in the arms race.

A second major theme of the new general secretary's foreign policy leadership is that strengthening the dilapidated Soviet economy is essential in order to guarantee and enhance the foundation of Soviet power abroad. As Gorbachev says, unless his generation reverses the internal decay of the last 10 years, the Soviet Union will not enter the 21st century as a great power worthy of the name. In large measure because he wants his country to have a growing, not a diminishing, role in the world outside, he has given domestic economic reform priority. Whether this means that Gorbachev merely seeks a breathing spell, or *peredyshka*, while he refurbishes Soviet power, expecting at some point in the future to resume the offensive, is a question that I will return to later.

Gorbachev joins the applause at the end of his five-hour opening speech to the 27th Party Congress in February 1986.

Continuity and Change

A noticeable feature of Soviet foreign policy in the Gorbachev era, at least up to this point, is its essential continuity with the past. The substance of policy has not changed to any great extent. There is no evidence of a new Soviet flexibility on issues that matter greatly to other major powers, with the exception of nuclear arms control. Soviet policy toward China has shifted, but the shift occurred in the post-1981 period under Leonid I. Brezhnev and his two immediate successors, Yuri V. Andropov and Konstantin U. Chernenko. Gorbachev has embroidered and advanced the process of normalizing Sino-Soviet relations, which had deteriorated sharply in the two decades before, but he did not invent the policy. Like his predecessors, Gorbachev seeks to ingratiate his country with America's major allies—both to secure leverage over the Americans and to erode whatever lingering sense of encirclement continues on the Soviet side—but without paying any compelling price. Like his predecessors, he continues to put the United States at the center of his concerns, subordinating most aspects of Soviet foreign policy to the needs of his U.S. policy. And where his predecessors had made material commitments, including economic and military aid, to such Third World countries as Afghanistan, Angola, Cuba, Ethiopia and Nicaragua, he has increased rather than reduced support while giving Third World relations a lower priority.

What has clearly changed is the style of Soviet policy under Gorbachev. From his skillfully conducted press conferences to his free-wheeling conversations with Western political leaders, from the velvet glove he has donned in dealing with the Japanese to the cooperation he has extended organizations like the International Atomic Energy Agency in the wake of the Chernobyl nuclear power plant disaster in April 1986, Gorbachev has altered the look of Soviet policy. He has brought a deftness to Soviet diplomacy that his predecessors had almost convinced the rest of the world was beyond their ken.

Is the change more than cosmetic? Does it reach beyond tactics and style to affect something truly substantial, such as the purposes of policy or the assumptions on which policy is based? Is the Soviet mind changing in ways that are important to the interests of the United States and its allies? Notwithstanding the continuity of Soviet foreign policy, the answer to all of these questions is yes.

Like other periods of accelerated conceptual adaptation—for example, Lenin's accommodation to the failure of the European revolution and Khrushchev's adjustment to the reality of nuclear weapons—Gorbachev's passage is of great potential significance. Only the first hints of the change are yet apparent, but if the evolution continues, the Gorbachev era will turn out to be one of the great turning points in the history of Soviet foreign policy.

Words, it will become apparent, are important. Words that carry with them new and different assumptions about modern international relations and the contest between East and West will become the precursors of altered deeds, indeed their source, rather than their counterpoint.

The current conceptual ferment did not spring into being on

the strength of Gorbachev's personality alone. As noted earlier, altered images of the world do not occur overnight. Meaningful change is usually a cumulative process. For more than a decade, members of the Soviet foreign policy establishment—intellectuals in the Soviet Academy of Sciences, the most sophisticated commentators in the media and the most talented members of the party and state foreign policy *apparat*—have been inventing and shaping ideas like those which Gorbachev now articulates. But he and the team he has collected around him are the first to permit such ideas to invade the conceptual world of the leadership.

At this early stage, nothing guarantees that the process must go forward, that it cannot be interrupted or thrown into reverse. Soviet leaders are talking about crucial matters in fresh ways, but their ideas are no more irreversible than is their hold on power. Even if their tenure continues, until word begins to merge with deed the new thinking will remain vulnerable to disappointment and impatience. It will be vulnerable, in addition, to those in the Soviet Union who see things in old ways and, indeed, to those in the West who do also.

Evidence of the new thinking can be traced in four areas: security, interdependence, relations with the Third World, and relations with other socialist nations. Taken together, these categories, which are the author's own, cut to the heart of the Soviet engagement in the outside world. Each dominates a crucial dimension of Soviet foreign policy. If the new thinking in each area were translated into concrete actions, it would significantly alter traditional Soviet behavior.

Security

In Gorbachev's reworked **concept of security,** two modifications are particularly salient. First, he has introduced a much broader and more diffuse notion of national security. A nation's security, he has been saying since early 1986, involves many elements, only some of which are military. In the modern world, national well-being, he argues, is often as much a matter of economic security as of military security; threats to stability are often as much political and economic as they are martial; and arms are often a poor and weak response to the security challenges facing the state. The theme he developed at the 27th Party Congress has become common in his discourse: "The character of contemporary weapons leaves no country with any hope of safeguarding itself solely with military and technical means, for example by building up a defense system, even the most powerful one. The task of ensuring security is increasingly a political problem to be resolved only by political means."

He is also the first Soviet leader to concede the link between national and mutual security. In a television address to the Soviet people in August 1986, he said, "Today one's own security cannot be ensured without taking into account the security of other states and peoples. There can be no genuine security unless it is equal for all and comprehensive. To think otherwise is to live in a world of illusions, in a world of self-deception." His reason is neither abstract nor excessively high-minded. As he had earlier explained to the 27th Party Congress, when others do not feel secure, "the fears and anxieties of the nuclear age generate unpredictability and concrete actions." By concrete actions he presumably had in mind, among other things, the nervous burst of arming to which the Americans had been moved by their reading of the Soviet Union's ongoing military efforts in the 1970s.

Interdependence

Gorbachev's second major conceptual contribution has been his notion of **interdependence** in international politics. Soviet leaders before him had used the phrase "the international division of labor." This concept gave the Soviet Union the excuse needed to participate in the capitalist-dominated international economic order and to seek removal of the West's discriminatory trade measures against the U.S.S.R. and its socialist allies. Gorbachev, however, employs the term in a much broader and more fundamental sense. Interdependence—when he speaks on the subject, he uses the word *vzaimozavisimost*—represents his conception of a basic dynamic in international relations.

Politics among nations, he seems to be arguing, have been transformed by the interweaving of societies and the emergence of problems exceeding the capacity of any nation or alliance of nations to solve autonomously. What he referred to at the international peace forum in Moscow in February 1987 as the "unprecedented diversity and at the same time growing interconnection and unity of the world" has turned an international setting once dominated by crudely competitive nations into a non-zero-sum game, one in which one side's loss is not necessarily the other side's gain. These are realities that, according to him, belittle the frontiers separating one society from another and setting one social system against another. These are realities, he comes close to saying, that also diminish the historic competition between East and West. Class struggle, the bedrock of Soviet theory, no longer has the sway that it once did. Gorbachev makes it compete with often crosscutting notions of what international politics are all about.

Third World

Gorbachev's third area of innovation concerns the **Third World** and the place he assigns it in contemporary Soviet policy. Conceptual ferment in this sphere involves the intermingling of several considerations. One senses that for Gorbachev and his colleagues the Third World has sunk lower among their priorities. Their attention is focused elsewhere, reflecting a tighter and more hard-nosed definition of Soviet interests. The Soviet Union under Gorbachev has not cut back economic and military commitments to Third World clients, and, in some old and in some innovative respects (for example, in southern Africa and the Middle East), it has even enlarged these commitments. But these issue forth from Moscow with no special expectations, few illusions, some impatience, and a clearly superior interest in other fields of endeavor.

Gorbachev's image of the critical dynamics within the Third World seems rather different from his predecessors', or, at least, from that with which Brezhnev worked in the 1970s. For Gorbachev the Third World has become a far less inviting place, one filled with headaches and troubles capable of embroiling the superpowers and spilling over to contaminate whole areas of foreign policy. It has also become unhappily a place where the Soviet Union spends more of its time these days defending embattled clients against counterrevolutionary onslaught than promoting the "national liberation struggle."

While his predecessors had already begun to absorb the fact that Soviet ventures in the Third World, like Soviet support for the Marxist government in Angola and for the Ethiopian side in the Ogaden War with Somalia, would disrupt relations with the United States, Gorbachev is really the first Soviet leader to begin grappling with what this realization means for any future détente with the Americans. To judge from the work of thoughtful specialists on the subject, he appreciates the need to address this problem in any serious future superpower dialogue, and he would admit that Soviet leaders can no longer skirt the issue as they did in the 1970s.

The deep and rather despairing Soviet sense of the obstacles to a far-reaching revolutionary transformation of the sociopolitical order within much of the Third World is hardly an original development in Gorbachev's time. For more than 10 years a Soviet awareness of the intractability of the problems facing developing countries has been growing and it has left Soviet leaders and elites with a powerful impression of the Third World as a hopeless and tragic arena, not a region of hope and promise.

Socialist Relations

If Gorbachev's evolving concept of security goes to the heart of East-West relations and, in particular, U.S.-Soviet relations; if his concept of interdependence touches on the essence of international politics; and if his concept of the Third World affects still another important sphere of Soviet foreign policy, the fourth area is in many ways the most fundamental of all. It is also the most recent one to undergo change and the one least demonstrably in ferment. The fourth category concerns the concepts that Gorbachev brings to the world of **socialist relations.**

With the Eurocommunists (chiefly Communist parties in Western Europe), his tendency has been to downplay the sources of ideological tension and to strike a pose of patience and broad-mindedness. When Alessandro Natta, the new general secretary of the Italian Communist party (PCI), was in Moscow in January 1986 on the first visit by a PCI general secretary in many years, Gorbachev's theme was that "we must look ahead to the future, taking into it only that which has stood the test of time and leaving behind, with no regrets, that which hinders us from working in a more cohesive and more efficient way." A year later, with Athos Fava, the general secretary of the Argentine Communist party, he was still more forthcoming. He spoke of the need to "overcome stereotypes that arose in the previous stage" among Communist parties and to "devise forms of cooperation based on equal rights and joint actions that are in keeping with the spirit of the times." He also, to Fava's delight, stressed that relations among Communist parties must "rule out any monopoly on truth" and any notion of a "center" within the socialist world.

How far the same tolerance goes in the case of the East Europeans is less clear. On the one hand, Gorbachev and his spokesmen pay homage to the reality, albeit not to the virtue, of diversity within the socialist "commonwealth." They pledge themselves to respect the right of their East European colleagues to find their own answers to their own problems. They even speak of the need to treat others' approaches to socialism as a genuinely important and valid contribution to the common store of knowledge. (In this context, it is noteworthy that some Soviet publications have gone out of their way to praise the economic and political reforms undertaken in Hungary.) On the other hand, to judge from Gorbachev's trip to Czechoslovakia in the spring of 1987, he is less and less hesitant to speak of the great experiment under way in the Soviet Union and to offer it as something of a parable. Significantly, however, under Gorbachev even oblique references to the so-called Brezhnev Doctrine of 1968, which declared the Soviet Union's right "to protect Communist regimes even if it means the use of force," have ceased, and East European leaders now appear to have more elbowroom than ever before, perhaps even in the sphere of foreign policy. Soviet experts who seem to hold views on Eastern Europe closest to Gorbachev's are beginning to offer remarkably bold analyses of the failure of economic integration among the socialist countries and of what must be done if these countries are to become part of the international economic order.

Together, these shifting perspectives on central issues of international politics contain the seeds of an important transformation of Soviet foreign policy. Should they continue to mature and then manifest themselves in a different Soviet way of doing things, scarcely any dimension of policy would remain unchanged. But what are the chances that these trends will continue to mature? Will they alter Soviet behavior? The answer to the first question depends only in part on Gorbachev's presence and rather more on developments outside the Soviet Union, including in particular the evolution of superpower relations. The answer to the second question has already begun to emerge.

Assessing Change

Mention the possibility that ideas on international politics are changing under Gorbachev and the response in many quarters in the West is, "Maybe, but until the change shows up in policy, I disbelieve." In fact, more change has occurred than many may have noticed. Take for example Soviet arms control initiatives over the last year. A few years ago, when in November 1983 Soviet negotiators ruined the talks on intermediate-range nuclear forces (INF) by walking out, a reasonable test for judging whether Soviet leaders were capable of new thinking would have been their readiness to accept the U.S. position on INF, to ameliorate the problem of fixed land-based intercontinental ballistic missile (ICBM) vulnerability by cutting the number of heavy Soviet missiles in half, and to resolve the problem of verification by accepting the principle of on-site inspection. Between October 1985 and March 1987, Gorbachev made each of these adjustments. In doing so, he wrenched traditional Soviet attitudes from their moorings. When the 1979–83 effort to forestall the modernization of the North Atlantic Treaty Organization's (NATO) theater nuclear forces failed, one Soviet commentator noted in *New Times*, "this generated disenchantment among many participants in the antimissile struggle." Some of the most disenchanted were clearly the Soviet leaders, as is obvious from his next sentence: "But at the time the inertia of the traditional 'tooth for a tooth' or 'missile for a missile' psychology was still strong among politicians. Historic changes were needed—the April plenary meeting of the CPSU [Communist party of the Soviet Union] Central Committee, the 27th CPSU Congress, and Reykjavik [Gorbachev's second summit meeting with President Ronald Reagan in October 1986]—to work out the really unconventional solutions which the new Soviet leadership now proposes to the world."

The Soviet appeal for observer status in the General Agreement on Tariffs and Trade (GATT), Soviet participation in the last meeting of the economic organization of the Pacific Basin Community in November 1986, and as an observer in the Asian Development Bank session in April 1987, and, more significantly, the awakened Soviet interest in the International Monetary Fund (IMF) represent other sharp modifications of long-standing policy. Western observers, in focusing on the problems that Soviet participation would pose for these institutions and the structural obstacles standing in the way of Soviet membership, are overlooking still more evidence of changing Soviet behavior.

A new Soviet willingness to join other countries in the struggle against terrorism and hints of a more enlightened approach to the global problems of food and population are further indications that Soviet conduct has already changed enough to raise the possibility that something of more profound consequence may be happening, that is, that basic Soviet assumptions may be changing.

The Meaning Behind the Changes

How one interprets the innovations in Soviet behavior and the airing of new ideas determines the importance that one attaches to them. The shifts can be put down to a variety of causes. Maybe, for example, they are simply the echo of the leadership's preoccupations at home and of a desire to be spared dangerous and demanding international diversions. Or maybe they reflect sheer expediency: All the talk about a radical approach to nuclear arms control may be no more than a device to do in the Strategic Defense Initiative (SDI, or Star Wars) and escape the need to compete with the Americans on a new technological frontier; talk of joining GATT may be no more than an effort to butter up the capitalist powers so that they might smile on Soviet efforts to attract their goods, services and capital.

Or maybe these shifts are simply a reaction to the clumsier features of the Brezhnev policy. In the party's international affairs apparat, one of the two principal deputies of Anatoly Dobrynin, the former Soviet ambassador to the United States, has confessed that Soviet policy in the late 1970s was "less than circumstance demanded—in large part, less flexible and less creative." Gorbachev himself is thought to believe his predecessors mishandled key challenges such as INF and relations with Afghanistan.

Unlike a fourth explanation, none of these lines of analysis suggests a very deep or lasting transformation of Soviet policy. The fourth explanation, however, takes the change far more seriously and traces its roots to trends emerging even before Gorbachev arrived on the scene. Although unnoticed by most Westerners, since the early 1970s Soviet academic analysts and, in less abstract forms, middle-level policymakers have been thinking fresh ideas on a host of issues—from the utility of force to the nature of strategic stability, from the role of alliances to the underlying changes in a bipolar international order. Therefore, many of the ideas to which Gorbachev lends high-level legitimacy had been gestating and developing long before he came to power and long before anyone began to stress the Soviet Union's crisis at home. They were ideas that took shape because of changing external realities, not because of domestic expediency, and, with or without Gorbachev, they are likely to continue to evolve and mature, although almost certainly not with the same force and vigor that he gives them.

Once more the problem is to distinguish between rhetoric and substance, to know which explanation or combination of explanations to accept. Whether there will be further melding of ideas and actions where important Soviet values are at stake will prove a fair though hard test of the new thinking. For example, if the Soviet Union does not merely flirt with the possibility of at last joining the IMF but alters domestic economic practices and institutions in order to be admitted, the reality of new concepts and their impact on behavior will be irrefutable. A decision by the Soviets to lift the secrecy surrounding their store of gold reserves, to forswear trade practices that amount to dumping, or, most tellingly, to begin moving toward currency convertibility would be a clear signal of a change in policy.

The Case for Candor

A different test—simple and yet profound—of a new and modern approach to foreign-policy making would be for the Soviets to be candid and open about foreign policy issues. Openness does not mean laying bare the workings of the policy-making process, but rather dealing frankly and honestly with the shortcomings and concerns of policy as such. As *Izvestiya*'s prominent commentator Alexander Bovin has lamented, foreign policy is the one area not touched by *glasnost,* that well-known Russian word that means openness and represents a freer flow of ideas and criticisms. Despite Foreign Minister Eduard Shevard-nadze's efforts last summer to shake foreign policy specialists from their lethargy and timidity, Soviet speeches and published analyses, on the whole, continue to present uncritical accounts of Soviet policy, in which the U.S.S.R. shares no blame when events go wrong, in which the misperception, incompetence and inflexibility are all on the other side. Soviet foreign policy analysts know this is not true, and in private they share far more balanced and realistic interpretations, but up to this time they are not permitted to print their views, except in pale Aesopian terms.

In a far more portentous area—namely security—the Soviets may already have begun to meet the rigorous test set out above. A transformation in the Soviet approach to the conventional military balance in Europe would be an indisputably consequential illustration of a shift in behavior that signifies a major adjustment of values. An argument can be made, and frequently is, that it is one thing for Soviet leaders to speak of a new concept of national security and of the link between national and mutual security. It is even one thing to reach an INF agreement with the United States on what are virtually American terms. (To many, Gorbachev's concessions on the INF agreement, signed in Washington in December 1987, merely represent an exceedingly clever way to denuclearize Western Europe and leave it exposed to Soviet conventional superiority.) But it is another thing actually to begin undoing the threat of offensively postured Soviet conventional forces in Central Europe. Were the Soviet Union to accept a regime depriving its forces of the ability to hammer through NATO's forward defenses and rapidly envelop the rear—giving up the so-called blitzkrieg strategy—there could be no denying the significance of the change. Concepts with immense implications for traditional (military) values of the Soviet Union would be at stake.

The intriguing fact is that Soviet thinking, in some quarters, appears suddenly to be evolving in this direction. For more than a year and a half, in various circles, including the general secretary's, the Soviets seem to have started to wrestle with the issue of conventional force restructuring—that is, not merely reducing conventional forces within the existing structure of the military balance, but altering their basic pattern of deployment.

As late as Gorbachev's January 15, 1986, speech on disarmament, the Soviet side still seemed to be operating within the old framework. But step-by-step since then Gorbachev has begun to introduce radically new ideas. At East Germany's 11th Party Congress in April 1986, he evoked the problem of the "confrontation on the [European] continent of mighty armed forces outfitted with conventional arms," arms whose "modern combat characteristics are drawing closer to systems of mass annihilation." He proposed that something be done to break out of the sterile and deadlocked framework of the mutual and balanced force reductions (MBFR) talks, extending the geographic zone of reductions to all of Europe "from the Atlantic to the Urals."

In June 1986, the Budapest proposal of the Warsaw Treaty Organization, also known as the Warsaw Pact, contained a reference to eliminating weapons particularly useful in a surprise attack. A month later, during French President François Mitterrand's Moscow visit, Gorbachev referred to West European fears of Soviet conventional superiority and said: "Let us look at all of this in a new way. For those types of weapons of which the West has more, let it make the corresponding reductions, and for those of which we have more, we will unhesitatingly eliminate this 'surplus.' In other words, let us look for balance at a lower level."

At the international forum in February 1987, he tied all these elements together and went one step beyond. "Take all our proposals. There are no weapons of ours that are not subject to negotiations," he began. "Our principle is simple: all armaments should be limited and reduced. . . . If there is any imbalance, we must restore the balance—not by letting the one short of some elements build them up, but by having the one with more of them scale them down." Then he went on: "It is important, in our view, while lowering the level of military confrontation, to carry through such measures as would make it possible to lessen, or better still, altogether exclude the possibility of surprise attack." And he added, in a way never quite done before, "The most dangerous *kinds of offensive weapons* must be removed from the zone of contact" (emphasis added).

Restudying Defense Postures

Important as these reformulations by Gorbachev are, they constitute only a part of a now rapidly developing picture. Over the last several months, parts of the Soviet academic community specializing in politico-strategic issues have begun to explore the practical implications for arms control of alternative defense postures in Europe. Within the military community, sometimes in collaboration with civilian coauthors, intellectuals have begun the process of reexamining military history—the standard method of introducing new ideas into the military—in ways justifying a more defensive, less offensive conventional force posture. Somewhere within the General Staff, according to private reports, officials are wrestling with the conceptual challenge of how the Soviet Union would have to alter weapons, deployments and operational doctrine to make compelling to NATO its claimed defensive purposes.

In May 1987, *New Times* published an interview with Brigadier Michael Harbottle, a retired British officer, who made the case for "nonprovocative defense," spelling out in detail the revision in deployments and hardware that would be required. A week earlier Polish leader General Wojciech Jaruzelski introduced his country's plan for European arms control and, in addition to many of the elements included earlier by Gorbachev, he added a proposal to alter military doctrine to make it less menacing. The theme was subsequently taken up at the June meeting of the Warsaw Pact Political Consultative Committee.

Two questions remain: Why would Gorbachev and the others change their minds in this fashion, implicitly sacrificing a clear military advantage? And what is the overarching significance of the change in terms of the question left unanswered early in this chapter: Is Gorbachev's new thinking only a momentary expedient, the quest for a breathing spell, or peredyshka, that will sooner or later give way to traditional aims and approaches?

If there is an explanation for the change in Gorbachev's view on conventional forces, it would appear to be his realization that he cannot direct the nuclear competition as he aspires to without addressing the conventional balance in Europe. Perhaps somewhere deep within his Soviet soul he still would like to see the nuclear and conventional balances decoupled, but the central reality of his day is that he cannot get the nuclear world he wants without coming to terms with the West's core security problem.

On the other leftover question: If Soviet leaders are seriously in the process of reconceiving their conventional defense requirements in Europe and increasingly prepared to contemplate an arms control regime that would refashion the military balance in Central Europe, this instance of new thinking alone would be of obvious enduring significance. Should this come to pass, it would be hard to argue that the new thinking was merely a device designed to secure the Soviet Union a momentary respite. Peredyshka or not, the Soviet Union would emerge as a fundamentally different challenge from what it has been in the past. In the end this will be the real test of the new thinking: whether the change affects the Soviet Union itself, not merely the strategy and tactics of an ongoing policy.

Subtle Shifts

The trouble is that those on the outside are not going to have an easy time deciphering the change under way. Partly the problem stems from the subtlety of what is taking place. To many in the West who will demand unambiguous proof that the leopard has changed its spots—"If Gorbachev's thinking were really changing, the Soviet Union would pull out of Afghanistan, or force the Vietnamese out of Kampuchea, or allow free emigration"—much of what is likely to happen will drift by unnoticed. For example, in Asia the Soviet approach may already be undergoing a very important transition, but it is of a nature sure to escape the attention of many.

For years the Soviet leadership has advanced the idea of an Asian collective security system and worked to draw reluctant Asian governments to the scheme. Gorbachev, too, speaks of a "comprehensive system of security" for the region. But in the earlier case the primary Soviet purpose was strategic and instrumental: to isolate, contain and pressure the Chinese. Gorbachev's concept appears to have an entirely different thrust: not so much to isolate the Chinese as to engage the Soviets. Brezhnev spoke of an Asian collective security system; Gorbachev speaks of a Helsinki-style conference on security and economic cooperation in Asia (with roles for China and the United States as great Pacific powers). Brezhnev had in mind the creation of military salients against the Chinese (and, indirectly, the Americans); Gorbachev stresses the economic enterprises in Asia of which the Soviet Union would like to be a part. But this tendency to move from a strategy of anti-Chinese containment to one of active Soviet engagement coexists with a comparatively inflexible approach to the contentious issues in Sino-Soviet and Soviet-Japanese relations and with a continuing strong military presence. Marbled realities of this sort are never easy to comprehend for those on the outside.

For a second reason observers will have difficulty knowing what to make of the change in progress. In almost any sphere that matters, change will come piecemeal, leaving outsiders to quarrel over its meaning and direction. To return to the key issue of European security and conventional force restructuring, which involves strong and deeply held values, particularly among the military, the process of translating a change in principle into refined, concrete concepts and *then* into a formal defense and arms control program will be slow, arduous and maybe contested.

Soviet negotiators are not likely to come to the next round of arms control talks in Europe with a comprehensive plan to undo their defense strategy and force posture of the last 40 years. They have scarcely begun to think through what Gorbachev's concessions in principle will mean in practice. For example, when asked what Gorbachev has in mind when he talks of removing the "most dangerous kinds of offensive arms" from Central Europe, Soviet politico-military analysts frankly confess the issue has hardly been addressed. While these same analysts maintain that, in the end, more than weapons systems will be involved (given the problem of distinguishing offensive from defensive arms) and, thus, that any real effort to deal with the problem will have to include deployments and operational strategy as well, none of this has yet assumed a distinctive shape.

In the meantime, political trial balloons, halting half-measures (say, a unilateral reduction of antiquated Soviet tanks) and an inchoate arms control posture are likely to be the best the Soviet leadership has to offer. Inevitably, many in the West will waste a good deal of time disputing the significance and value of these measures, in the process neglecting to probe and test the larger, slower-moving evolution of which they may be a timid part.

Finally, the new thinking is different from glasnost and similar notions in a way that also will not facilitate Western comprehension. Glasnost and the other words serve political ends at home. Their implementation depends overwhelmingly on Soviet leaders, elites and public. But Gorbachev never suggested the new thinking was for the Soviet Union only. On the contrary, when he

Gorbachev and Reagan at the Reykjavik, Iceland, summit in October 1986.

Terry Arthur
The White House

appeals for new thinking on the nature of security, the role of nuclear weapons and the character and impact of interdependence, he is addressing himself to the West as well.

Challenge for Western Leaders

As noted earlier, Gorbachev's new ideas represent to a degree his accommodation to the requirements of a changing international setting, but they are not utterly disconnected from the evolution of the West's own response to the same requirements. How far and fast he is prepared to go will depend in part on Western governments. Skeptical Western leaders who start by doubting the prospect of any real change in Soviet perspectives, who expect unreasonable one-way Soviet concessions as proof of sincerity and who themselves cling to unreconstructed notions of national security and the East-West contest have it within their power to retard the Soviet Union's further adaptation.

From this derives the first counsel to the Western policymaker: Contrary to the instincts of many in the policy community, skepticism and disbelief these days are not a prudent point of departure for policy toward Gorbachev's Soviet Union. Uncertainty, yes, because one cannot know with confidence how far the change will go. But naysaying and reflexive doubt are an unsound, perhaps even a reckless, base for policy. They will leave Western governments forever reacting to Soviet initiatives and viewed by their publics as hidebound and closed to the possibility of reforming East-West relations. Second, and more important, if, as growing evidence suggests, the Soviet leadership has begun to rethink the premises of its foreign policy, the West's tendency to disbelieve will make it harder for it to recognize and reinforce the change under way. More perniciously, it will also blind the West, as almost certainly it already has, to policy adjustments that are the result of these shifting premises.

Were the skepticism that marks the Reagan Administration's approach to Gorbachev to give way to the agnosticism more characteristic of the West Europeans, there would still remain a fundamental problem. Some wisely counsel the West, as did West German Foreign Minister Hans-Dietrich Genscher in February 1986, to test Gorbachev's intentions. But there is no way to test Gorbachev without testing ourselves. Safe tests are preposterous tests: undo the Berlin Wall, take the bulk of Soviet forces out of Eastern Europe, transform the Soviet political system. More meaningful tests face the West with risks. Drawing the Soviet Union into a serious effort to restructure the conventional military balance in Europe will entail putting on the line important elements of NATO's force posture. Working out constraints on the use of Soviet military power in Third World conflicts will mean the United States, too, must be ready to tie its hands in some measure.

No Western government, indeed no Western political party, has begun to think through the process of testing Gorbachev, let alone the challenge of maintaining cohesion within the Western alliance as the process goes forward. Worse, no important political figure or group has even begun to formulate the standards we would want Gorbachev to meet. The truth is no Western government, beginning with the United States, knows what it wants from the Soviet Union at this point—certainly not well enough to convey it to its people and allies.

The third piece of advice is to engage the Soviet Union. Every U.S. Administration from John F. Kennedy's to the present has described the U.S.-Soviet relationship as both competitive and cooperative, requiring strength and resolve, on the one hand, and flexibility and a readiness for dialogue, on the other. In short, from Kennedy to Reagan, U.S. leadership has claimed to follow a two-track policy toward the Soviet Union. The trouble is that since the late stages of the Carter Administration it has been two-track in rhetoric only. The one track—strengthening the military, demonstrating toughness, applying sanctions and the like—has been vigorously pursued; the other—looking for over-lapping areas of common interest, fashioning stronger arms control regimes, expanding economic and other practical forms of cooperation—has been a subordinate and neglected element of policy.

A strong and self-confident America need not fear, indeed dare not avoid, engaging the Soviet Union. Engaging the Soviet Union means not cold-shouldering its leaders when they express interest in observer status in international economic institutions like GATT. It means taking them seriously when they suggest a larger role for international peacekeeping operations with super-power support and a smaller role for direct superpower interven-tion. It means substituting greater economic cooperation for political warfare by economic means.

More essentially, it means risking an earnest and relatively open-minded dialogue with Gorbachev and his colleagues over the kind of strategic nuclear regime we are prepared to build together, not impose unilaterally; over the refashioning of the conventional military balance in Europe; over the role of the superpowers in areas of explosive conflict, minus the double standard of the current U.S. Administration; and over the place of the centrally planned economies in a troubled international economic order. But, from the start, built into this dialogue there should be active negotiations seeking manageable accords, which draw strength from the dialogue and restore momentum to it. These should not be confined to the sphere of arms control. Managing the U.S.-Soviet relationship is a broader and more diffuse proposition than arms control alone. Until the two sides engage one another not merely on arms control questions but in those spheres that proved so lethal to détente in the 1970s, those spheres where power was not simply accumulated but used, there is small chance of revising the U.S.-Soviet rivalry. And until the American side tests Gorbachev on a more profound and imaginative level than it has to this point, an important, maybe a historic opportunity will be wasted.

Implications of the 'New Thinking' for the United States*
by the Task Force

Recent signs of important changes in Soviet thinking about domestic and foreign affairs pose important new challenges and opportunities. Taken together with major reforms being undertaken in most other European socialist countries, these changes call for a process of policy reexamination in the West and a new dialogue between East and West on ways to create a more stable and cooperative relationship.

These changes in the East have not yet been fully responded to by the West. It is increasingly clear that they represent more than a change in style or rhetoric. What then are the implications of these changes for Western policy? How should America and its allies respond to Gorbachev's challenge?

With this in mind, the New York-based Institute for East-West Security Studies, an independent European-American public policy research center, convened a bipartisan 38-member Task Force of prominent Americans to examine the content and policy

---

*Excerpted from the report of the Task Force on Soviet New Thinking.

HIGHLIGHTS OF U.S.-SOVIET

Soviet leaders	STALIN	MALENKOV/ BULGANIN/ KHRUSHCHEV	KHRUSHCHEV
Soviet events		Sputnik ●	Sino-Soviet split ● ● 20th Party Congress; Khrushchev's anti-Stalin speech
New arms control era	■ U.S. drops first atomic bomb, on Hiroshima ■ U.S. Baruch Plan for international control of nuclear resources ■ Soviet's first A-bomb test	■ International Atomic Energy Agency	Limited Test Ban Treaty ■ U.S.-Soviet "Hot Line" ■
	1945	1950	1955	1960
East-West milestones	▼ NATO ▼ Yugoslav opposition to Stalin ▼ UN Charter ▼_____ ▼ Berlin blockade	▼ Warsaw Treaty Organization (Warsaw Pact) ▼ Suez Canal crisis Khrushchev visits U.S. ▼ ▼ Korean War ▼ Invasion of Hungary	▼ Bay of Pigs ▼ Cuban missile crisis ▼ Berlin Wall
Summits	◆ Yalta ◆ Potsdam	◆ Geneva Camp David ◆	◆ Paris (cancelled because of U2 incident) ◆ Vienna
U.S. leaders	TRUMAN	EISENHOWER	JFK

32

RELATIONS, 1945-1988

OSYGIN/ EZHNEV	BREZHNEV	ANDROPOV/ CHERNENKO/ GORBACHEV

● Brezhnev Doctrine claiming the Soviet Union's right to protect Communist regimes, with force, if necessary.

27th Party Congress ●

■ Nuclear Non-proliferation Treaty

■ START and INF negotiations begin

Biological and toxin ■ weapons ban

Soviet walkout from INF-START talks ■

SALT II Talks ■   ■ Vladivostok accords

INF Treaty ■

■ SALT II Treaty signed

Helsinki conference ■___■

Stockholm agreement ■

SALT I Talks ■_____■ ABM Treaty

■ U.S. Strategic Defense Initiative (SDI)

■ Outer Space Treaty

■ Mutual and Balanced Force Reductions talks begin

1965	1970	1975	1980	1985-88	

Soviets, Cubans to Angola ▼

▼ U.S. boycotts Moscow Olympics

U.S. invasion of Grenada ▼

Soviet invasion of Afghanistan ▼

▼ Soviets boycott L.A. Olympics

▼ Soviet invasion of Czechoslovakia

▼ Polish crisis

▼ U.S. escalates role in Vietnam War

▼ U.S. pulls out of Vietnam

U.S. trade sanctions ▼

◆ Glassboro

◆ Moscow

Geneva ◆

◆ Moscow

◆ Vienna

◆ Vladivostok

Reykjavik ◆

Washington ◆

◆ Helsinki

Washington ◆

JOHNSON	NIXON	FORD	CARTER	REAGAN	

implications of the new thinking and propose policy recommendations. The Task Force's key findings, as summarized in the final report, follow.

In the face of domestic economic stagnation, widespread social apathy and a widening technological gap vis-à-vis the West, Soviet General Secretary Mikhail Gorbachev has undertaken the most far-reaching revamping of the Soviet system in over half a century. While the Soviet Union remains a closed Communist society, Gorbachev has challenged a whole series of ingrained practices and attitudes, from strictly centralized economic management to an often militarized foreign policy, which has been the basis for Soviet policy since Stalin's time. In foreign affairs, he has introduced new concepts and new flexibility into Soviet diplomacy. Yet the West has not come to terms with these changes.

Balancing Soviet power and maintaining a strong Western alliance remain central to U.S. national interests. By the same token, the United States and its allies have a long-term interest in encouraging the moderation of Soviet power. Because the Soviet Union is a global power, Gorbachev's initiatives demand an active response by the United States and its Western allies. In many areas, from arms control to emigration, the Soviet Union has begun to make changes in directions long advocated by the West. While far from complete, these changes present new opportunities, and challenges, which the West should not ignore. The Task Force strongly recommends that the United States and its Western allies welcome the reformist tendencies that Gorbachev has set in motion and encourage those which promote a moderation of Soviet power. Toward that end, the United States and its allies should engage the Soviet Union in an effort to explore possibilities for agreement and resolve key points of tension.

A purely reactive Western approach in the face of the new Soviet policy is not an acceptable option, the Task Force believes. Western policies as well as Gorbachev's domestic policy priority are bound to affect Soviet foreign policy. There is considerable uncertainty about the long-term success of Gorbachev's reforms. Nevertheless, over time, the new course chosen by Gorbachev will affect the ways in which the Soviet Union carries out its role as a superpower. A more subtle and flexible Soviet diplomacy requires the West to develop a broader and more active policy toward the Soviet Union, including standards to define and meet common security requirements in a rapidly changing international environment. Failure to do so would sacrifice the diplomatic initiative to the Soviet Union as well as abdicate U.S. responsibility to future generations to pursue prospects for substantially improving relations between East and West.

What Is Changing in Soviet Foreign and Domestic Policy?

The West needs to think anew about specific changes the Soviet Union has made in its own policies. Many of these changes are only beginnings and ultimate Soviet intentions remain unclear, but it is important to note that some of them move toward long-standing Western preferences:

● *Arms Control*—The U.S.S.R. adopted the Western proposal of a zero option on the INF issue. In addition, the U.S.S.R. has moved toward the Western positions on verification, including on-site inspection. It has also raised the prospect of asymmetrical conventional force reductions in Central Europe. It has accepted the principle of deep reductions in offensive strategic weapons and proposed a concept of "sufficiency" in military forces.

● *Role of the Military*—There has been a reduction in the Soviet military's role and influence in the highest policymaking councils, and Gorbachev has made clear to the military that they have to accept spending restraints and greater openness in the dissemination of military information.

● *The International Economy*—Gorbachev has placed special emphasis on reducing Soviet autarky by increasing trade, joint ventures, and expressing an interest in cooperating with such major international organizations as GATT.

● *The Domestic Economy*—Gorbachev has initiated a major decentralization of operational responsibility for the economy, and he clearly intends to move toward more flexible, modern, and efficient economic planning and management. He has admitted the inadequacy of Soviet statistics and called for more-accurate economic information.

● *Human Rights*—In the fields of culture and dissent, Gorbachev has displayed a degree of openness and toleration unthinkable just three years ago. In the area of emigration, the change has been less dramatic, but Gorbachev has increased the emigration of Soviet Jews, ethnic Germans and other groups. While glasnost has a long way to go, it has clearly led to progress on human rights, which have been a major concern of the West.

● *Regional Issues*—While Gorbachev has as yet made no significant effort to scale back existing Soviet global commitments, he has given a lower priority to the military expansion of Soviet interests in the Third World than his predecessors.

● *Eastern Europe*—While urging closer and more "efficient" economic integration, Gorbachev has permitted a somewhat more flexible expression of specific national interests in Eastern Europe than his predecessors.

Agenda for Action

The Task Force recommends that as first steps Western policy choices focus on five key areas:

● *Security Issues*—The United States and its NATO allies should intensify talks with the Warsaw Pact aimed at reducing conventional forces and eliminating offensive strike potentials, particularly those designed for surprise attack. Given the geographical differences and existing force imbalances, new approaches must include asymmetrical reductions of forward-based armored units, which present the greatest threat of surprise attack.

Both sides need to move rapidly to conclude an agreement on deep cuts in strategic offensive nuclear forces. These reductions should be designed to enhance strategic stability and eliminate the capacity to launch a crippling first strike. At the same time, both sides need to find ways to strengthen the ABM [Antiballistic Missile] Treaty and to ensure that any research on strategic defensive systems is consistent with preservation of the treaty.

The West should push for a rapid conclusion of the global Geneva chemical weapons negotiations, including the establishment of an international verification regime. Such an agreement would help increase confidence in Europe at a time when some are concerned over the implications of the elimination of medium- and shorter-range nuclear missiles from the Continent.

● *International Economic Issues*—Except in a precisely defined area of strategic technologies, which entails tighter, more efficient regulations on the part of the Coordinating Committee (COCOM), composed of representatives of NATO countries, expanded East-West trade is in the U.S. interest. The West should welcome Soviet efforts to develop the legal foundation for a system of equitable joint ventures. While Western governments should not subsidize credits, neither should they oppose the extension of private credit through normal commercial rates and practices to the Soviet Union. The prospect of observer status in the GATT and IMF should be used to encourage greater openness and information about the Soviet economy.

If the Soviet Union demonstrates heightened respect for human rights, the U.S. government and Congress should consider bringing their policy in congruence with U.S. allies by reevaluating the Jackson-Vanik and Stevenson amendments restricting trade with and credit to the U.S.S.R. The West should aim to normalize the framework for trade with all Warsaw Treaty countries, on the basis of mutual and reciprocal interests.

In addition, the U.S.-Soviet umbrella agreements on scientific and technological cooperation should be revived and expanded, on the basis of full reciprocity.

● *Human Rights*—The West should welcome increased glasnost while continuing to make clear to the Soviet government that its observance of internationally recognized human rights is the mark of a civilized power and a condition for truly collaborative relations between the Soviet Union and the West. The West should insist that the Soviet Union fully live up to the commitments it undertook under the Helsinki Final Act to encourage the freer movement of people, ideas and information across international boundaries.

● *Regional Issues*—In Afghanistan, the West must continue to make clear that Soviet occupation of that country poses strict limits to genuine collaboration between the U.S.S.R. and the

A Soviet withdrawal from Afghanistan, where the mujahideen have been waging war against the invaders for over eight years, would signal a real change in Gorbachev's thinking, many analysts believe.

© Ludmilla Thorne

West. Conversely, a rapid Soviet withdrawal, with sufficient international guarantees, would be a forceful demonstration that the new political thinking has specific policy implications.

In other areas of conflict which could lead to possible super-power confrontation—such as Central America, southern Africa, and the Persian Gulf—the West should intensify discussions aimed at clarifying interests and creating conditions for greater stability. Within this framework, U.S.-Soviet meetings on regional issues should be upgraded as part of a regularized summit process. The purpose would be to seek solutions to these problems in conjunction with other concerned parties.

In the Arab-Israeli dispute, the United States and U.S.S.R. should work together to advance a peace process which guarantees the territorial integrity and interests of all states and parties.

● *Political Dialogue*—U.S.-Soviet summit meetings, as well as meetings at other governmental and nongovernmental levels, should be held on a regular basis.

Conclusion

The West must have no illusions about the need to balance Soviet power, but neither should it overlook opportunities to encourage the Soviet Union to be a more responsible and integrated member of the international community. Although the long-term success of Gorbachev's policy remains uncertain, the process he has launched holds out a promise of a further moderation of Soviet power and an opportunity to develop and institutionalize areas of cooperation in the East-West relationship. Some in the West worry about giving the Soviet Union a breathing spell. They fear that Gorbachev's economic reforms will simply strengthen the U.S.S.R. in the long run. But Soviet economic and social problems will not be quickly solved. In the meantime, greater openness and pluralization should be welcomed for their own sake as well as for the effect they can have in moderating the way Soviet power is used.

In order to seize the opportunities offered by new Soviet policies, the United States and its allies need to respond creatively to Gorbachev's initiatives. In order to do that, the West must be clear about its own policy objectives and priorities. New political thinking in the East requires new policy thinking in the West.

APPENDIX

Basic Aims and Directions of the Party's Foreign Policy Strategy*
by Mikhail Gorbachev

Comrades,

The tasks underlying the country's economic and social development also determine the CPSU's strategy in the world arena. Its main aim is crystal clear—to provide the Soviet people with the possibility of working under conditions of lasting peace and freedom. Such, in essence, is the party's primary program requirement of our foreign policy. To fulfill it in the present situation means, above all, to terminate the material preparations for nuclear war.

After having weighed all the aspects of the situation that has taken shape, the CPSU has put forward a coherent program for the total abolition of weapons of mass destruction before the end of this century, a program that is historic in terms of its dimensions and significance. Its realization would open for mankind a fundamentally new period of development and provide an opportunity to concentrate entirely on constructive labor.

As you know, we have addressed our proposals not only through the traditional diplomatic channels but also directly to world public opinion, to the peoples. The time has come to realize thoroughly the harsh realities of our day: nuclear weapons harbor a hurricane which is capable of sweeping the human race from the face of the earth. Our address further underscores the open, honest, Leninist character of the CPSU's foreign policy strategy.

---

*Text from the *Political Report of the CPSU Central Committee to the 27th Party Congress,* delivered February 25, 1986, by Mikhail Gorbachev (Moscow, Novosti Press Agency Publishing House, 1986). Bold type is as it appears in the Novosti edition. Minor changes in style, punctuation and spelling have been made for consistency.

Strengthening Peace

Socialism unconditionally rejects war as a means of settling political and economic contradictions and ideological disputes among states. Our ideal is a world without weapons and violence, a world in which each people freely chooses its path of development, its way of life. This is an expression of the humanism of Communist ideology, of its moral values. That is why for the future as well the **struggle against the nuclear threat, against the arms race, for the preservation and strengthening of universal peace** remains the fundamental direction of the party's activities in the international arena.

There is no alternative to this policy. This is all the more true in periods of tension in international affairs. It seems that never in the decades since the war has the situation in the world been so explosive, and consequently complex and uncongenial, as in the first half of the 1980s. The right-wing group that came to power in the United States and its main NATO fellow travelers made a steep turn from détente to a policy of military strength. They have adopted doctrines that reject good neighborly relations and cooperation as principles of world development, as a political philosophy of international relations. The Washington Administration remained deaf to our calls for an end to the arms race and an improvement of the situation.

Perhaps it may not be worth churning up the past? Especially today when in Soviet-U.S. relations there seem to be signs of a change for the better, and realistic trends can now be detected in the actions and attitudes of the leadership of some NATO nations. We feel that it is worthwhile, for the drastic frosting of the international climate in the first half of the 1980s was a further reminder that nothing comes of itself: peace has to be fought for, and this has to be a persevering and purposeful fight. We have to look for, find, and use even the smallest opportunity in order—while this is still possible—to reverse the trend toward an escalation of the threat of war. Realizing this, the Central Committee of the CPSU at its April [1985] Plenary Meeting once again analyzed the character and dimensions of the nuclear threat and defined the practical steps that could lead to an improvement of the situation. We were guided by the following considerations of principle.

First. The character of present-day weapons leaves ... [no] country ... [any] hope of safeguarding itself solely with military and technical means, for example, by building up a defense system, even the most powerful one. The task of ensuring security is increasingly seen as a political problem, and it can only be resolved by political means. In order to progress along the road of disarmament what is needed is, above all, the will. Security cannot be built endlessly on fear of retaliation, in other words, on the doctrines of "containment" or "deterrence." Apart from the absurdity and amorality of a situation in which the whole world becomes a nuclear hostage, these doctrines encourage an arms race that may sooner or later go out of control.

Second. In the context of the relations between the U.S.S.R. and the United States, security can only be mutual, and if we take international relations as a whole it can only be universal. The highest wisdom is not in caring exclusively for oneself, especially to the detriment of the other side. It is vital that all should feel equally secure, for the fears and anxieties of the nuclear age generate unpredictability in politics and concrete actions. It is becoming extremely important to take the critical significance of the time factor into account. The appearance of new systems of weapons of mass destruction steadily shortens time and narrows down the possibilities for adopting political decisions on questions of war and peace in crisis situations.

Third. The U.S. military-industrial machine remains the locomotive of militarism, for so far it has no intention of slowing down. This has to be taken into consideration, of course. But we are well aware that the interests and aims of the military-industrial complex are not at all the same as the interests and aims of the American people, as the actual national interests of that great country.

Naturally, the world is much larger than the United States and its occupation bases on foreign soil. And in world politics one cannot confine oneself to relations with only one, even a very important, country. As we know from experience, this only promotes the arrogance of power. Needless to say, we attach considerable significance to the state and character of the relations between the Soviet Union and the United States. Our countries coincide on quite a few points, and there is the objective need to live in peace with each other, to cooperate on a basis of equality and mutual benefit, and on this basis alone.

Fourth. The world is in a process of swift changes, and it is not within anybody's power to maintain a perpetual status quo in it. It consists of many dozens of countries, each having perfectly legitimate interests. All without exception face a task of fundamental significance: without neglecting social, political and ideological differences all have to master the science and art of restraint and circumspection on the international scene, to live in a civilized manner, in other words, under conditions of civil international intercourse and cooperation. But to give this cooperation wide scope there has to be an all-embracing system of international economic security that would in equal measure protect every nation against discrimination, sanctions, and other attributes of imperialist, neocolonialist policy. Alongside disarmament such a system can become a dependable pillar of international security in general.

In short, the modern world has become much too small and fragile for wars and a policy of strength. It cannot be saved and preserved if the way of thinking and actions built up over the centuries on the acceptability and permissibility of wars and armed conflicts are not shed once and for all, resolutely and irrevocably.

No Winner in Arms Race

This means . . . [it must be realized] that it is no longer possible to win an arms race, or nuclear war for that matter. The continuation of this race on earth, let alone its spread to outer space, will accelerate the already critically high rate of stockpiling and perfecting nuclear weapons. The situation in the world may assume such a character that it will no longer depend upon the intelligence or will of political leaders. It may become captive to technology, to technocratic military logic. Consequently, not only nuclear war itself but also the preparations for it, in other words, the arms race, **the aspiration to win military superiority can, speaking in objective terms, bring no political gain to anybody.**

Further, this means understanding that the present level of the balance of the nuclear potentials of the opposite sides is much too high. For the time being it ensures **equal danger** to each of them. But only for the time being. Continuation of the nuclear arms race will inevitably heighten this equal threat and may bring it to a point where even parity will cease to be a factor of military-political deterrence. Consequently, it is vital, in the first place, greatly to reduce the level of military confrontation. In our age, genuine equal security is guaranteed not by the highest possible, but by the lowest possible, level of strategic parity, from which nuclear and other types of weapons of mass destruction must be totally excluded.

Lastly, this means realizing that in the present situation there is no alternative to cooperation and interaction between all countries. Thus, the objective—I emphasize, objective—conditions have taken shape in which confrontation between capitalism and socialism can proceed **only and exclusively in forms of peaceful competition and peaceful contest.**

For us peaceful coexistence is a political course which the U.S.S.R. intends to go on following unswervingly, ensuring the continuity of its foreign policy strategy. The CPSU will pursue a vigorous international policy stemming from the realities of the world we live in. Of course, the problem of international security cannot be resolved by one or two, even very intensive, peace campaigns. Success can only be achieved by consistent, methodical and persevering effort.

Continuity in foreign policy has nothing in common with a simple repetition of what has been done, especially in tackling the problems that have piled up. What is needed is a high degree of accuracy in assessing one's own possibilities, restraint, and an exceptionally high sense of responsibility when decisions are made. What is wanted is firmness in upholding principles and stands, tactical flexibility, a readiness for mutually acceptable compromises, and an orientation on dialogue and mutual under-standing rather than on confrontation.

Moscow's Move

As you know, we have made a series of unilateral steps—we put a moratorium on the deployment of intermediate-range missiles in Europe, cut back the number of these missiles, and stopped all nuclear explosions. In Moscow and abroad there have been talks with leaders and members of the governments of many countries. The Soviet-Indian, Soviet-French and Soviet-U.S. summits were necessary and useful steps.

The Soviet Union has made energetic efforts to give a fresh impetus to the negotiations in Geneva, Stockholm and Vienna, the purpose of which is to curb the arms race and strengthen confidence between states. Negotiations are always a delicate and complex matter. Of cardinal importance here is to make an effort to achieve a mutually acceptable balance of interests. To turn weapons of mass destruction into an object of political scheming is, to say the least, immoral, while in political terms this is irresponsible.

Lastly, concerning our statement of January 15 of this year, taken as a whole our program is essentially an alloy of the philosophy of shaping a safe world in the nuclear-space age with a platform of concrete actions. The Soviet Union offers approaching the problems of disarmament in their totality, for in terms of security they are linked with one another. I am not speaking of rigid linkages or attempts at "giving way" in one direction in order to erect barricades in another. What I have in mind is a plan of concrete actions strictly measured out in terms of time. The U.S.S.R. intends to work perseveringly for its realization, re-garding it as the **central direction of its foreign policy for the coming years.**

The Soviet military doctrine is also entirely in keeping with the letter and spirit of the initiatives we have put forward. Its orientation is unequivocally defensive. In the military sphere we intend to act in such a way as to give nobody grounds for fears, even imagined ones, about their security. But to an equal extent we and our allies want to be rid of the feeling that we are threatened. The U.S.S.R. undertook the obligation not to be the first to use nuclear weapons and it will abide strictly by that obligation. But it is no secret that scenarios for a nuclear strike against us do exist. We have no right to overlook this. The Soviet Union is a staunch adversary of nuclear war in any variant. Our country stands for removing weapons of mass destruction from use, for limiting the military potential to reasonable adequacy. But the character and level of this ceiling continue to be restricted by the attitudes and actions of the United States and its partners in the blocs. Under these conditions we repeat again and again: **the Soviet Union lays no claim to more security, but it will not settle for less.**

Verification All-important

I should like to draw attention to the problem of verification, to which we attach special significance. We have declared on several occasions that the U.S.S.R. is open to verification, that we are interested in it as much as anybody else. All-embracing, strictest verification is perhaps the key element of the disarmament process. The essence of the matter, in our opinion, is that **there can be no disarmament without verification and that verification without disarmament makes no sense.**

There is yet another matter of principle. We have stated our attitude to Star Wars quite substantively. The United States has already drawn many of its allies into this program. There is the danger that this state of things may become irreversible. Before it is too late, it is imperative to find a realistic solution **guaranteeing that the arms race does not spread to outer space.** The Star Wars program cannot be permitted to be used as a stimulus for a further arms race or as a roadblock to radical disarmament. Tangible progress in what concerns a drastic reduction of nuclear potentials can be of much help in surmounting this obstacle. For that reason the Soviet Union is ready to make a substantial step in that direction, to resolve the question of intermediate-range missiles in the European zone separately—without linking it to problems of strategic armaments and outer space.

The Soviet program has touched the hearts of millions of people, and among political leaders and public personalities, interest in it continues to grow. The times today are such that it is hard to brush it off. The attempts to sow doubt in the Soviet Union's constructive commitment to accelerate the solution of the pressing problem of our day—the destruction of nuclear weapons—and to tackle it in practical terms are becoming less and less convincing. Nuclear disarmament should not be the exclusive domain of political leaders. The whole world is now pondering over this, for it is a question of life itself.

Disarmament's Friends and Foes

But, also, it is necessary to take into account the reaction of the centers of power that hold in their hands the keys to the success or failure of disarmament negotiations. Of course, the U.S. ruling class, to be more exact its most egoistical groups linked to the military-industrial complex, have other aims that are clearly opposite to ours. For them disarmament spells out a loss of profits and a political risk, for us it is a blessing in all respects—economically, politically and morally.

We know our principal opponents and have accumulated a complex and extensive experience in our relations and talks with them. The day before yesterday, we received President Reagan's reply to our statement of January 15. The U.S. side began to set forth its considerations in greater detail at the talks in Geneva. To be sure, we shall closely examine everything the U.S. side has to say on these matters. However, since the reply was received literally on the eve of the Party Congress, the U.S. Administration apparently expects, as we understand it, that our attitude to the U.S. stand will be made known to the world from this rostrum.

What I can say right away is that the President's letter does not give ground for amending in any way the assessment of the international situation as had been set forth in the report before the reply was received. The report says that the elimination of nuclear arms is the goal all the nuclear powers should strive for. In his letter the President agrees in general with some . . . [of the]

other Soviet proposals and intentions as regards the issues of disarmament and security. In other words, the reply seems to contain some reassuring opinions and statements.

However, these positive pronouncements are drowning in various reservations, "linkages" and "conditions" which in fact block the solution of radical problems of disarmament. Reduction in the strategic nuclear arsenals is made conditional on our consent to the Star Wars program and reductions, unilateral, by the way, in Soviet conventional arms. Linked to this are also problems of regional conflicts and bilateral relations. The elimination of nuclear arms in Europe is blocked by the references to the stand taken by Britain and France and the demand to weaken our defenses in the eastern part of the country, while the U.S. military forces in that region remain as they are. The refusal to stop nuclear tests is justified by arguments to the effect that nuclear weapons serve as a factor of "deterrence." This is in direct contradiction with the purpose reaffirmed in the letter—the need to do away with nuclear weapons. The reluctance of the United States and its ruling circles to embark on the path of nuclear disarmament manifests itself most clearly in their attitude to nuclear explosions, the termination of which is the demand of the whole world.

To put it in a nutshell, it is hard to detect in the letter we have just received any serious readiness by the U.S. Administration to get down to solving the cardinal problems involved in eliminating the nuclear threat. It looks as if some people in Washington and elsewhere, for that matter, have got used to living side by side with nuclear weapons—linking with them their plans in the international arena. However, whether they want it or not, the Western politicians will have to answer the question: Are they prepared to part with nuclear weapons at all?

In accordance with an understanding reached in Geneva there will be another meeting with the U.S. President. The significance that we attach to it is that it ought to produce practical results in key areas of limiting and reducing armaments. There are at least two matters on which an understanding could be reached: the cessation of nuclear tests and the abolition of U.S. and Soviet intermediate-range missiles in the European zone. And then, as a matter of fact, if there is readiness to seek agreement, the question of the date of the meeting would be resolved of itself: We will accept any suggestion on this count. But there is no sense in empty talks. And we shall not remain indifferent if the Soviet-U.S. dialogue that has started and inspired some not-unfounded hopes of a possibility for changes for the better is used to continue the arms race and the material preparations for war. It is the firm intention of the Soviet Union to justify the hopes of the peoples of our two countries and of the whole world who are expecting from the leaders of the U.S.S.R. and the United States concrete steps, practical actions, and tangible agreements on how to curb the arms race. We are prepared for this.

Border Security

Naturally, like any other country, we attach considerable importance to the security of our frontiers, on land and at sea. We have many neighbors, and they are different. We have no territorial claims on any of them. We threaten none of them. But as experience has shown time and again, there are quite a few persons who, in disregard of the national interests of either our country or those of countries neighboring upon us, are endeavoring to aggravate the situation on the frontiers of the Soviet Union.

For instance, counterrevolution and imperialism have turned Afghanistan into a bleeding wound. The U.S.S.R. supports that country's efforts to defend its sovereignty. We should like, in the nearest future, to withdraw the Soviet troops stationed in Afghanistan at the request of its government. Moreover, we have agreed with the Afghan side on the schedule for their phased withdrawal as soon as a political settlement is reached that will ensure an actual cessation and dependably guarantee the nonresumption of foreign armed interference in the internal affairs of the Democratic Republic of Afghanistan. It is in our vital national interest that the U.S.S.R. should always have good and peaceful relations with all its neighbors. This is a vitally important objective of our foreign policy.

The CPSU regards the **European direction** as one of the main directions of its international activity. Europe's historic opportunity and its future lie in peaceful cooperation among the nations of that Continent. And it is important, while preserving the assets that have already been accumulated, to move further: from the initial to a more lasting phase of détente, to mature détente, and then to the building of dependable security on the basis of the Helsinki process and a radical reduction of nuclear and conventional weapons.

The significance of the **Asian and Pacific direction** is growing. In that vast region there are many tangled knots of contradictions and, besides, the political situation in some places is unstable. Here it is necessary, without postponement, to search for the relevant solutions and paths. Evidently, it is expedient to begin with the coordination and then the pooling of efforts in the interests of a political settlement of painful problems so as . . . to at least take the edge off the military confrontation in various parts of Asia and stabilize the situation there.

This is made all the more urgent by the fact that in Asia and other continents the **flashpoints of military danger** are not being extinguished. We are in favor of vitalizing collective quests for ways of defusing conflict situations in the Middle East, Central America, southern Africa, in all of the planet's turbulent points. This is imperatively demanded by the interests of general security.

Crises and conflicts are fertile soil also for international terrorism. Undeclared wars, the export of counterrevolution in all forms, political assassinations, the taking of hostages, the highjacking of aircraft, and bomb explosions in streets, airports and railway stations—such is the hideous face of terrorism, which its instigators try to mask with all sorts of cynical inventions. The U.S.S.R. rejects terrorism in principle and is prepared to cooperate actively with other states in order to uproot it. The Soviet Union will resolutely safeguard its citizens against acts of violence and do everything to defend their lives, honor and dignity.

Looking back over the past year one will see that, by all the evidence, the prerequisites for improving the international situation are beginning to form. But prerequisites for a turn are not the turn itself. The arms race continues and the threat of nuclear war remains. However, international reactionary forces are by no means omnipotent. The development of the world revolutionary process and the growth of mass democratic and antiwar movements have significantly enlarged and strengthened the **huge potential of peace, reason and good will.** This is a powerful counterbalance to imperialism's aggressive policy.

The destinies of peace and social progress are now linked more closely than ever before with the dynamic character of the **socialist-world system's economic and political development.** The need for this dynamism is dictated by concern for the welfare of the peoples. But for the socialist world it is necessary also from the standpoint of counteraction to the military threat. Lastly, it helps demonstrate the potentialities of the socialist way of life. We are watched by both friends and foes. We are watched by the huge and heterogeneous world of developing nations. It is looking for its choice, for its road, and what this choice will be depends to a large extent on socialism's successes, on the credibility of its answers to the challenges of time.

We are convinced that socialism can resolve the most difficult problems confronting it. Of vital significance for this is the increasingly vigorous interaction whose effect is not merely the adding up but the multiplication of our potentials and which serves as a stimulus for common advancement. This is reflected also in joint documents of countries of the socialist community.

Interaction between governing Communist parties remains the heart and soul of the **political cooperation** among these countries. During the past year there has been practically no fraternal country with whose leaders we have not had meetings and detailed talks. The forms of such cooperation are themselves being updated. A new and perhaps key element, the multilateral working meetings of leaders of fraternal countries, is being established. These meetings allow for prompt and friendly consultations on the entire spectrum of problems of socialist construction, on its internal and external aspects.

In the difficult international situation the prolongation of the **Warsaw Treaty** by a unanimous decision of its signatories was of great significance. This treaty saw its second birth, so to speak, and today it is hard to picture world politics as a whole without it. Take the Sofia conference of the treaty's Political Consultative Committee. It was a kind of threshold of the Geneva dialogue.

In the **economic sphere** there is now the Comprehensive Program of Scientific and Technological Progress. Its importance lies in the transition of the Council for Mutual Economic Assistance (CMEA) countries to a coordinated policy in science and technology. In our view, changes are also required in the work of the very headquarters of socialist integration—the CMEA. But the main thing is that in carrying out this program there is less armchair administration and fewer committees and commissions of all sorts, that more attention is given to economic levers, initiative and socialist enterprise, and that work collectives are drawn into this process. This would indeed be a party approach to such an extraordinary undertaking.

Socialist World Relations

Vitality, efficiency and initiative—all these qualities meet the requirements of the times, and we shall strive to have them spread throughout the system of relations between fraternal parties. The CPSU attaches growing significance to live and broad communication between citizens of socialist countries, between people of different professions and different generations. This is a source of mutual intellectual enrichment, a channel for exchanges of views, ideas and the **experience of socialist construction.** Today it is especially important to analyze the character of the socialist way of life and understand the processes of perfecting democracy, management methods and personnel policy on the basis of the development of several countries rather than of one country. A considerate and respectful attitude to each other's experience and the employment of this experience in practice are a huge potential of the socialist world.

Generally speaking, one of socialism's advantages is its ability to learn: to learn to resolve the problems posed by life; to learn to forestall the crisis situations that our class adversary tries to create and utilize; to learn to counter the attempts to divide the socialist world and play off some countries against others; to learn to prevent collisions of the interests of different socialist countries, harmonize them by mutual effort, and find mutually acceptable solutions even to the most intricate problems.

It seems to us that it is worth taking a close look also at the relations in the socialist world as a whole. We do not see the community as being separated by some barrier from other socialist countries. The CPSU stands for honest, aboveboard relations with all Communist parties and all countries of the world socialist system, for comradely exchanges of opinion between them. Above all, we endeavor to see what unites the socialist world. For that reason the Soviet Communists are gladdened by every step toward closer relations among all socialist states, by every positive advance in these relations.

One can say with gratification that there has been a measure of improvement of the Soviet Union's relations with its great neighbor—**socialist China.** The distinctions in attitudes, in particular to a number of international problems, remain. But we also note something else—that in many cases we can work jointly, cooperate on an equal and principled basis, without prejudice to third countries.

There is no need to explain the significance of this. The Chinese Communists called the victory of the U.S.S.R. and the forces of progress in World War II a prologue to the triumph of the people's revolution in China. In turn, the formation of [the] People's [Republic of] China helped to reinforce socialism's positions in the world and disrupt many of imperialism's designs and actions in the difficult postwar years. In thinking of the future, it may be said that the potentialities for cooperation between the U.S.S.R. and China are enormous. They are great because such cooperation is in accordance with the interests of both countries; because what is dearest to our peoples—socialism and peace—is indivisible.

The CPSU is an inalienable component of the international Communist movement. We, the Soviet Communists, are well aware that every advance we make in building socialism is an advance of the entire movement. For that reason the CPSU sees its primary internationalist duty in ensuring our country's successful progress along the road opened and blazed by the October Revolution.

The Communist movement in the nonsocialist part of the world remains the principal target of political pressure and persecution by reactionary circles of the bourgeoisie. All the fraternal parties are constantly under fire from anti-Communist propaganda, which does not scruple to use the most despicable means and methods. Many parties operate underground, in a situation of unmitigated persecution and repressions. Every step the Communists take calls for struggle and personal courage. Permit me, comrades, on behalf of the 27th Congress, on behalf of the Soviet Communists, to express sincere admiration for the dedicated struggle of our comrades, and profound fraternal solidarity with them.

In recent years the Communist movement has come face-to-face with many new realities, tasks and problems. There are all indications that it has entered upon a qualitatively new phase of development. The international conditions of the work of Communists are changing rapidly and profoundly. A substantial restructuring is taking place in the social pattern of bourgeois society, including the composition of the working class. The problems facing our friends in the newly independent states are not simple. The scientific and technological revolution is exercising a contradictory influence on the material condition and consciousness of working people in the nonsocialist world. All this requires the ability to do a lot of reappraising and demands a bold and creative approach to the new realities on the basis of the immortal theory of Marx, Engels and Lenin. The CPSU knows this well from its own experience.

The Communist movement's immense diversity and the tasks that it encounters are likewise a reality. In some cases this leads to disagreements and divergences. The CPSU is not dramatizing the fact that complete unanimity among Communist parties exists not always and not in everything. Evidently, there generally cannot be an identity of views on all issues without exception. The Communist movement came into being when the working class entered the international scene as an independent and powerful political force. The parties that comprise it have grown on national soil and pursue common-end objectives—peace and socialism. This is the main, determining thing that unites them.

We do not see the diversity of our movement as a synonym for disunity, much as unity has nothing in common with uniformity, hierarchy, interference by some parties in the affairs of others, or the striving of any party to have a monopoly over what is right. The Communist movement can and should be strong by virtue of its class solidarity, of equal cooperation among all the fraternal parties in the struggle for common aims. This is how the CPSU understands unity and it intends to do everything to foster it.

The trend toward strengthening the potential of peace, reason and good will is enduring and, in principle, irreversible. At the back of it is the desire of people of all nations to live in concord and to cooperate. However, one should look at things realistically: The balance of strength in the struggle against war is taking shape in the course of an acute and dynamic confrontation between progress and reaction. An immutable factor is the CPSU's solidarity with the forces of national liberation and social emancipation, and our course toward close interaction with socialist-oriented countries, with revolutionary-democratic parties, and with the Nonaligned Movement. The Soviet public is prepared to go on promoting links with non-Communist movements and organizations, including religious organizations that are against war.

This is also the angle from which the CPSU regards its relations with the **social democratic movement.** It is a fact that the ideological differences between the Communists and the social democrats are deep, and that their achievements and experience are dissimilar and nonequivalent. However, an unbiased look at the standpoints and views of each other is unquestionably useful to both the Communists and the social democrats, useful in the first place for furthering the struggle for peace and international security.

Building International Security

We are living in a world of realities and are building our international policy in keeping with the specific features of the present phase of international development. A creative analysis of this phase and vision of prospects have led us to a conclusion that is highly significant. Now, as never before, it is important to find ways for closer and more productive cooperation with governments, parties, and mass organizations and movements that are genuinely concerned about the destinies of peace on earth with all peoples in order to **build an all-embracing system of international security.**

We see the fundamental principles of this system in the following:

1. In the military sphere

● renunciation by the nuclear powers of war—both nuclear and conventional—against each other or against third countries;

● prevention of an arms race in outer space, cessation of all nuclear weapons tests and the total destruction of such weapons, a ban on and the destruction of chemical weapons, and renunciation of the development of other means of mass annihilation;

● a strictly controlled lowering of the levels of military capabilities of countries to limits of reasonable sufficiency;

● disbandment of military alliances, and as a stage toward this—renunciation of their enlargement and of the formation of new ones;

● balanced and proportionate reduction of military budgets.

2. In the political sphere

● strict respect in international practice for the right of each people to choose the ways and forms of its development independently;

● a just political settlement of international crises and regional conflicts;

● elaboration of a set of measures aimed at building confidence between states and the creation of effective guarantees against attack from without and of the inviolability of their frontiers;

● elaboration of effective methods of preventing international terrorism, including those ensuring the safety of international land, air and sea communications.

3. In the economic sphere

● exclusion of all forms of discrimination from international practice; renunciation of the policy of economic blockades and sanctions if this is not directly envisaged in the recommendations of the world community;

● joint quest for ways for a just settlement of the problem of debts;

● establishment of a new world economic order guaranteeing equal economic security to all countries;

● elaboration of principles for utilizing part of the funds released as a result of a reduction of military budgets for the good of the world community, of developing nations in the first place;

● the pooling of efforts in exploring and making peaceful use of outer space and in resolving global problems on which the destinies of civilization depend.

4. In the humanitarian sphere

● cooperation in the dissemination of the ideas of peace, disarmament and international security; greater flow of general objective information and broader contact between peoples for the purpose of learning about one another; reinforcement of the spirit of mutual understanding and concord in relations between them;

● extirpation of genocide, apartheid, advocacy of fascism and every other form of racial, national or religious exclusiveness, and also of discrimination against people on this basis;

● extension—while respecting the laws of each country—of international cooperation in the implementation of the political, social and personal rights of people;

● decision in a humane and positive spirit of questions related to the reuniting of families, marriage and the promotion of contacts between people and between organizations;

● strengthening of and quests for new forms of cooperation in culture, art, science, education and medicine.

These principles stem logically from the provisions of the program of the CPSU. They are entirely in keeping with our concrete foreign policy initiatives. Guided by them it would be possible to make peaceful coexistence the highest universal principle of relations between states. In our view, these principles could become the point of departure and a sort of guideline for a direct and systematic dialogue—both bilateral and multilateral—among leaders of countries of the world community.

And since this concerns the destinies of peace, such a dialogue is particularly important among the permanent members of the [UN] Security Council—the five nuclear powers. They bear the main burden of responsibility for the destinies of humankind. I emphasize—not a privilege, not a foundation for claims to "leadership" in world affairs, but responsibility, about which nobody has the right to forget. Why then should their leaders not gather at a **roundtable** and discuss what could and should be done to strengthen peace?

As we see it, the entire existing mechanism of arms-limitation negotiations should also start to function most effectively. We must not "grow accustomed" to the fact that for years these talks have been proceeding on a parallel course, so to speak, with a simultaneous buildup of armaments.

The U.S.S.R. is giving considerable attention to a joint examination, at international forums as well as within the framework of the Helsinki process, of the world economy's problems and prospects, the interdependence between disarmament and development, and the expansion of trade and scientific and technological cooperation. We feel that in the future it would be important to convene a **World Congress on Problems of Economic Security** at which it would be possible to discuss as a package everything that encumbers world economic relations.

We are prepared to consider seriously any other proposal aimed in the same direction.

Under all circumstances success must be achieved in the battle to prevent war. This would be an epoch-making victory of the whole of humanity, of every person on earth. The CPSU sees active participation in this battle as the essence of its foreign policy strategy.

Talking It Over

A Note for Students and Discussion Groups

This issue of the HEADLINE SERIES, like its predecessors, is published for every serious reader, specialized or not, who takes an interest in the subject. Many of our readers will be in classrooms, seminars or community discussion groups. Particularly with them in mind, we present below some discussion questions—suggested as a starting point only—and references for further reading.

Discussion Questions

Do you believe Soviet foreign policy has changed significantly? If so, how, and in which areas? If not, what would constitute a significant change in Soviet behavior? Refer to Afghanistan, nuclear and conventional arms control, the Arab-Israeli conflict, Central America, East-West economic ties.

What do you think caused the shifts in Soviet foreign policy under Gorbachev?

Do you think the changes now under way in Soviet foreign policy are reversible? If so, what could set back the course of reform? What could accelerate it?

What is the relationship between Soviet internal reforms and Soviet foreign policy?

What are United States interests when it comes to reform in Soviet domestic and foreign policy? Can the United States affect the course of reform in the Soviet Union? If so, how?

Some Western policymakers believe that the changes Gorbachev has set in motion hold out the prospect for a transformation of the East-West relationship. Do you agree?

In what areas of Soviet foreign policy would change be most significant for the United States and its allies? Are significant changes required in U.S. foreign policy?

What do you think should be the major directions in U.S.-Soviet relations in the years ahead?

How do you think a Soviet citizen sees American policy? Refer to SDI, East-West trade restrictions, the Middle East, U.S.-China relations, the human rights issue.

READING LIST

Dallin, Alexander, "Gorbachev's Foreign Policy and the 'New Political Thinking' " in *Gorbachev's Reforms: U.S. and Japanese Assessments,* edited by Peter Juviler and Hiroshi Kimura. Hawthorne, N.Y., Aldine de Gruyter, 1988.

Gorbachev, Mikhail, *Perestroika: New Thinking for Our Country and the World.* New York, Bessie-Harper & Row, 1987. The Soviet leader's own assessment of the necessity for change, written mainly for an American readership.

How Should America Respond to Gorbachev's Challenge? A Report of the Task Force on Soviet New Thinking. New York, Institute for East-West Security Studies, 1987. A bipartisan panel of 38 American academics, business leaders and government officials assesses Soviet "new thinking" and appropriate Western responses.

Implications of Soviet New Thinking. New York, Institute for East-West Security Studies, 1987. U.S. Senator Bill Bradley (D-N.J.), West German Foreign Minister Hans-Dietrich Genscher, East German Foreign Minister Harry Ott, U.S. Deputy Secretary of State John C. Whitehead discuss Soviet "new thinking" and its implications for East-West security.

Larrabee, F. Stephen, and Lynch, Allen, "Gorbachev: The Road to Reykjavik." *Foreign Policy,* No. 65, Winter 1986-87. A cautious but optimistic overview of welcome developments in Soviet foreign policy during Gorbachev's first two years.

Lynch, Allen, *The Soviet Study of International Relations.* Cambridge, England, Cambridge University Press, 1987. Roots of Soviet "new thinking" explored in the writings of Soviet specialists in international relations.

Maynes, Charles William, "America's Chance." *Foreign Policy,* No. 68, Fall 1987. Recommendations for exploiting the opportunity Gorbachev represents for U.S. foreign policy.

Political Report of the CPSU Central Committee to the 27th Party Congress. Delivered by Mikhail Gorbachev, February 25, 1986. Moscow, Novosti Press Agency Publishing House, 1986.

Simes, Dimitri, "Gorbachev: A New Foreign Policy?" *Foreign Affairs,* Vol. 65, No. 3 (*America and the World 1986*). An early, skeptical look at change in Gorbachev's foreign policy.

"The Soviet Union: Gorbachev's Reforms." *Great Decisions 1988,* pp. 37–47. New York, Foreign Policy Association, 1988.

The Foreign Policy Association

Since 1918, the Foreign Policy Association's purpose has been to help Americans gain a better understanding of significant issues in U.S. foreign policy and stimulate constructive and informed citizen participation in world affairs.

FPA is independent, nonpartisan and nongovernmental. It is a national, not-for-profit, educational organization whose major function is to define and call wide public attention to those major issues of contemporary foreign policy which government and people must resolve in democratic partnership.

Americans from all walks of life take part in FPA-sponsored meetings with national and world leaders, and in study and discussion programs based on FPA publications. The annual Great Decisions program, based on the briefing book prepared by FPA's editors, involves more than 250,000 Americans in study and discussion of eight of the most important foreign policy issues facing the United States. The year-round HEADLINE SERIES *books and special FPA publications bring lively, authoritative resources on current world topics to the general public, to educators and other professionals, and to students in high schools, colleges and universities. And the wider debate and comment FPA's publications stimulate through TV, radio and the print media reach out to more Americans than any other world affairs educational service in the nation.*

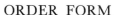

ORDER FORM

Please send me:

_____ copies of GREAT DECISIONS 1988 .... $8.00 each
_____ copies of A CITIZEN'S GUIDE TO U.S.
      FOREIGN POLICY .... $7.95 each
/   / a copy of FPA's catalogue of publications .... free

Name _____
                          (please print)
Address _____

_____

City _____ State _____ Zip _____

- Prepayment must accompany all orders of $8.00 or less, plus postage and handling.
- Prepayment must accompany all orders from individuals.
- Educational institutions, businesses or libraries can be billed for orders above $8.00 if purchase order is received.
- All bulk orders within the U.S. will be shipped UPS.
- Please add postage and handling to your order as follows:

Orders up to $8.00 .... $1.50
Orders from $8.01 to $30.00 .... $2.00
Orders from $30.01 to $60.00 .... $3.00
Orders above $60.00 .... $5.00

Please make checks payable to: Foreign Policy Association
Allow three to four weeks for delivery.

Mail to: Foreign Policy Association
           729 Seventh Avenue
           New York, NY 10019
           (212) 764-4050

DATE DUE